My first SEA ANIMALS

scan this code:

Dolphin

Fish

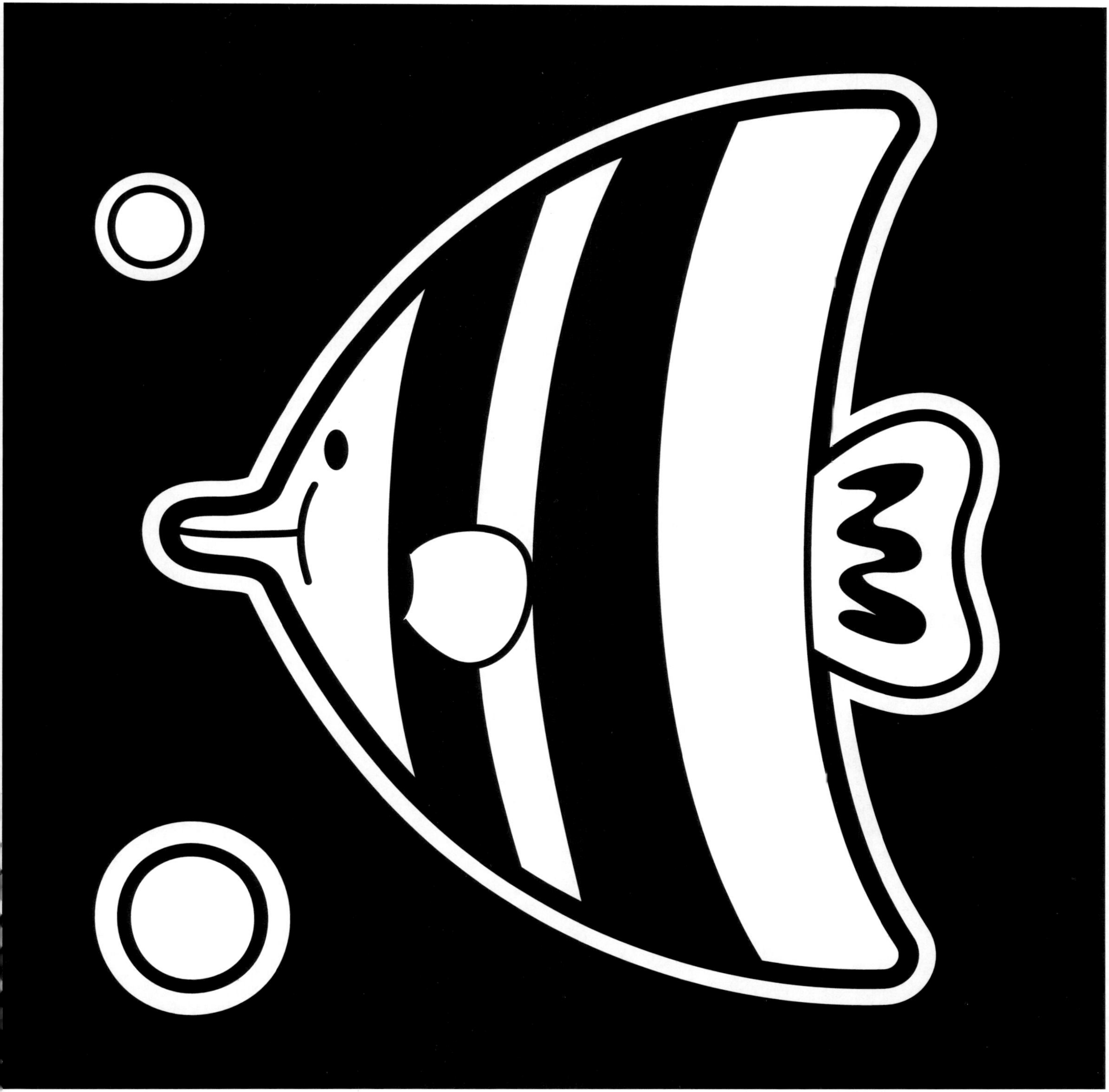

Turtle

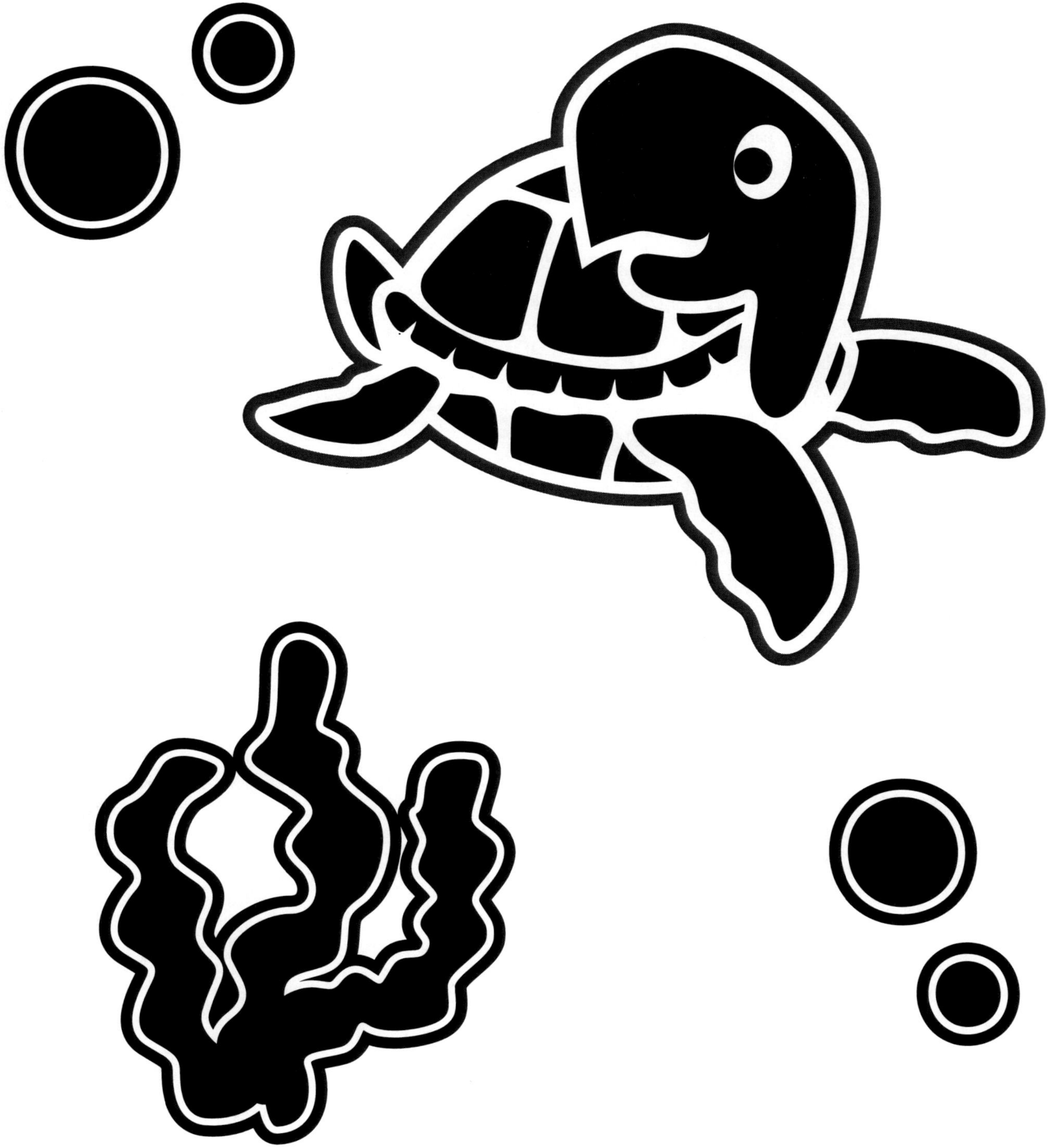

Manatee

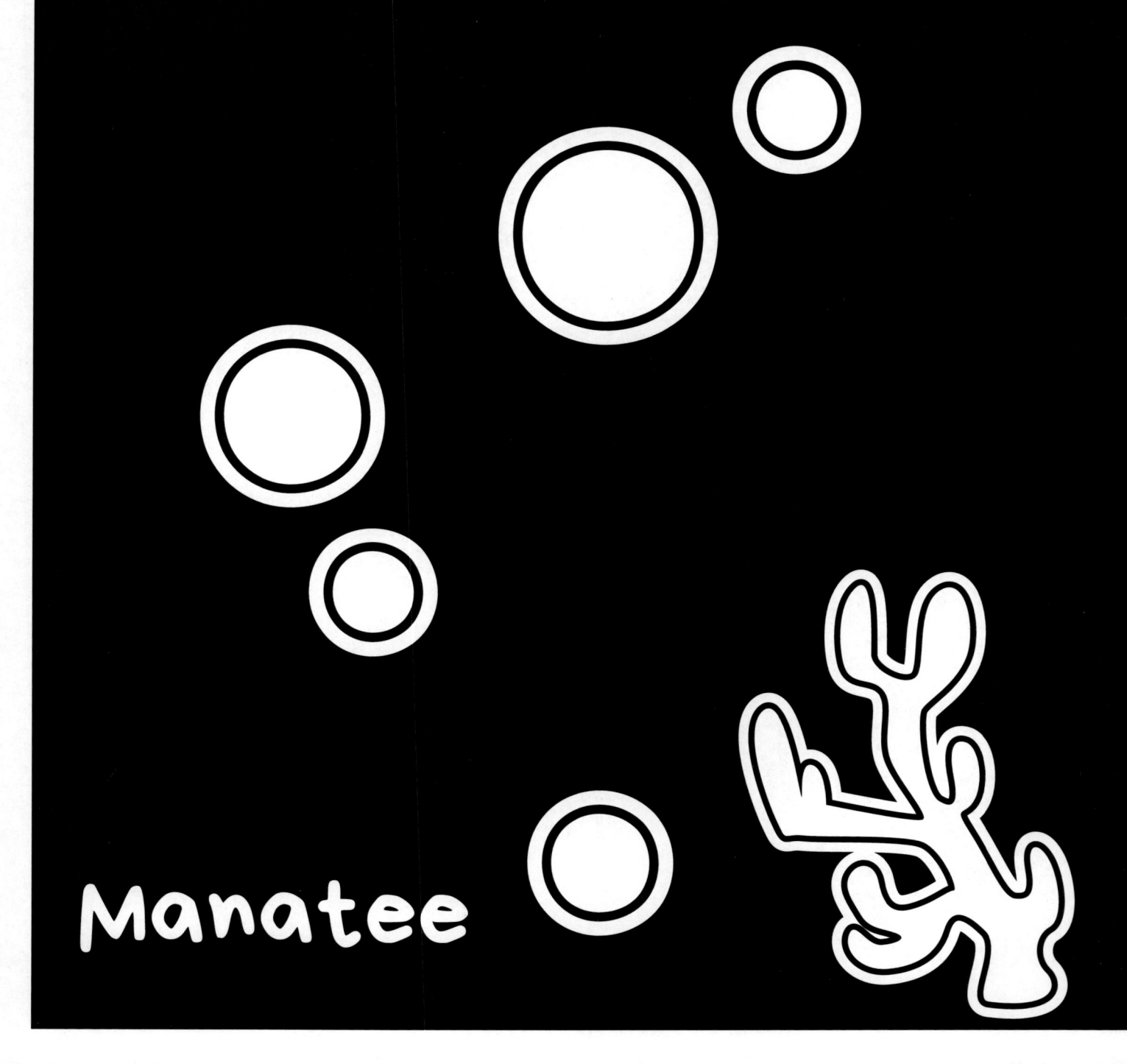

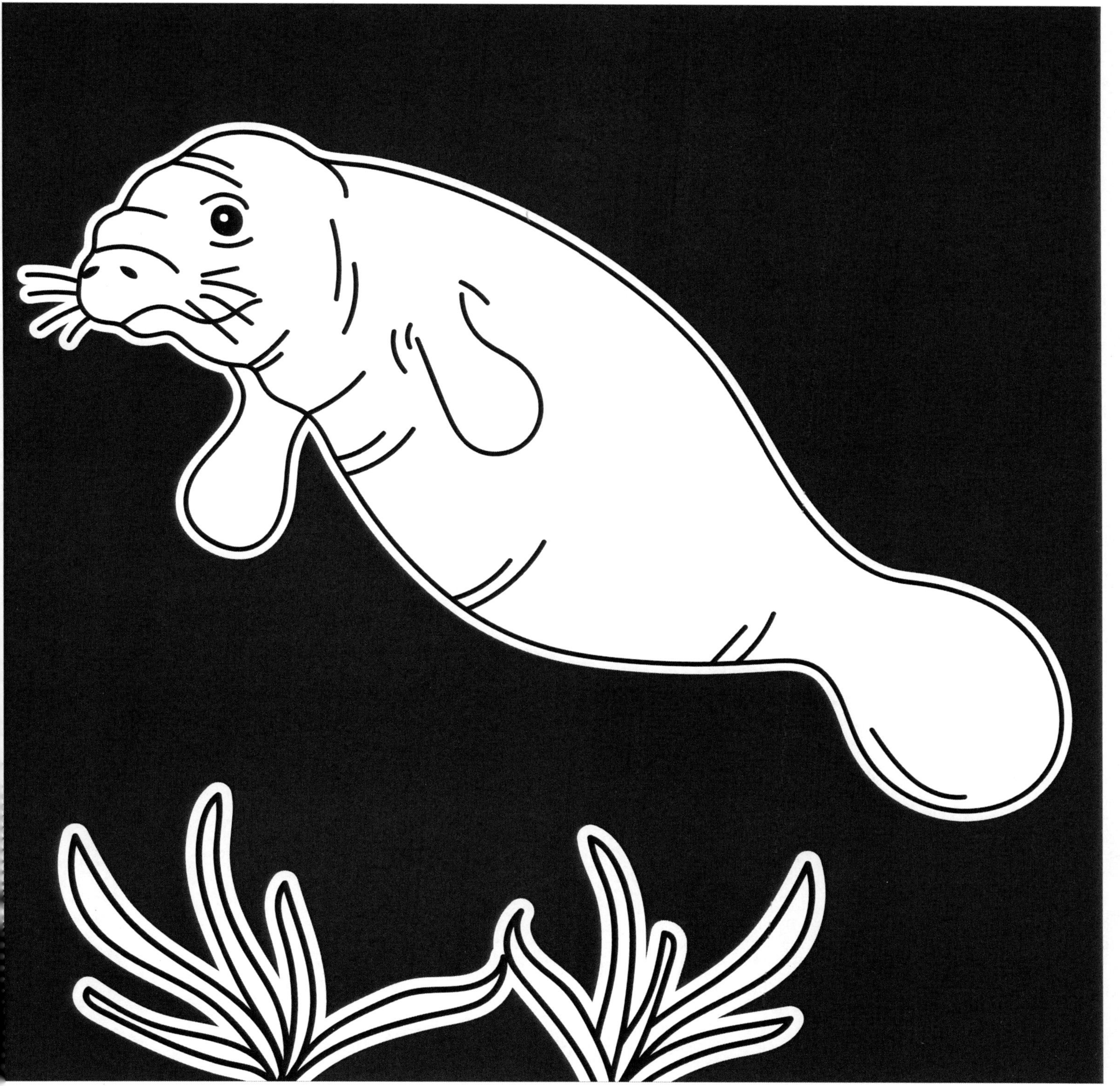

Octopus

Seahorse

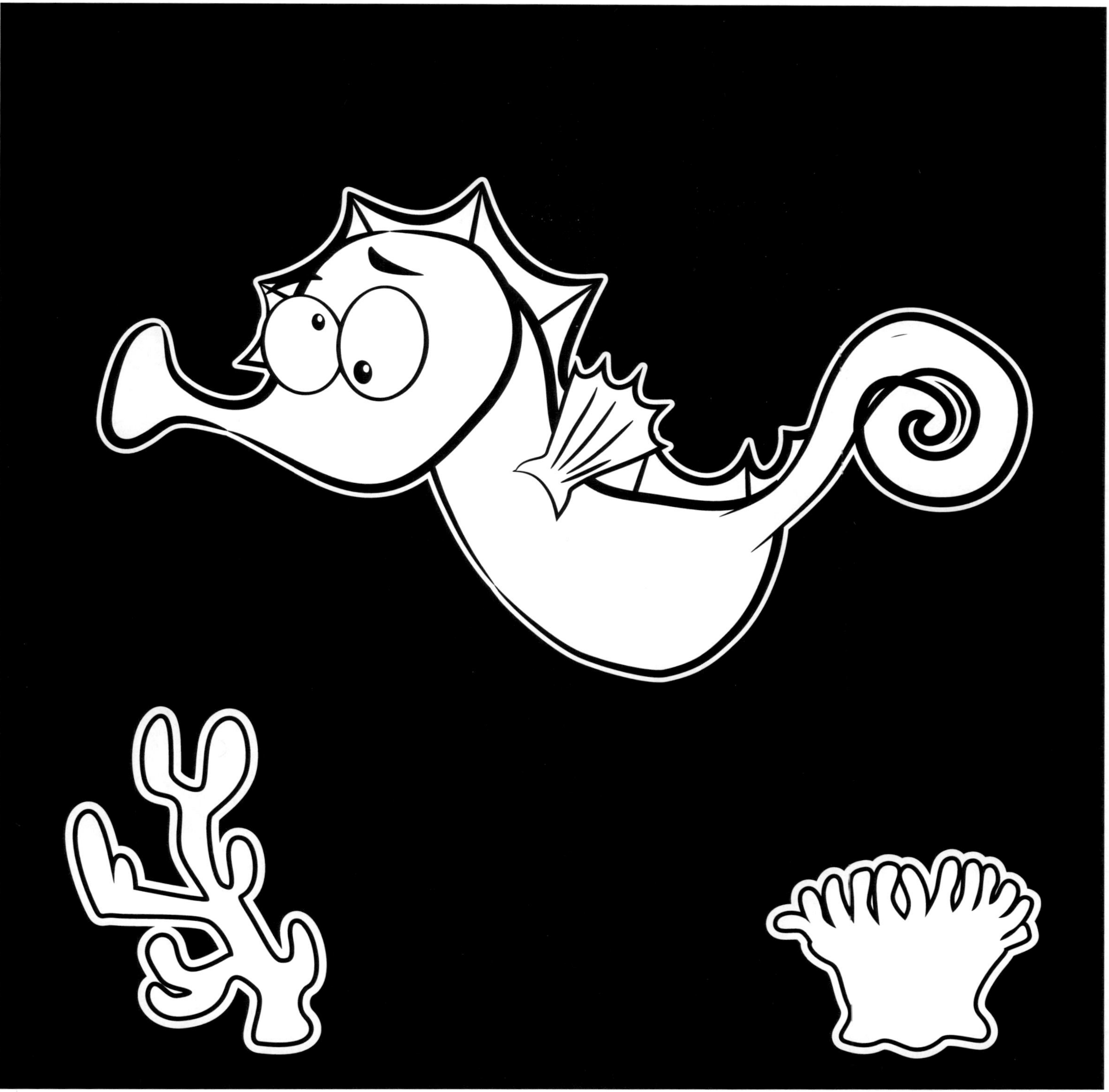

Crab

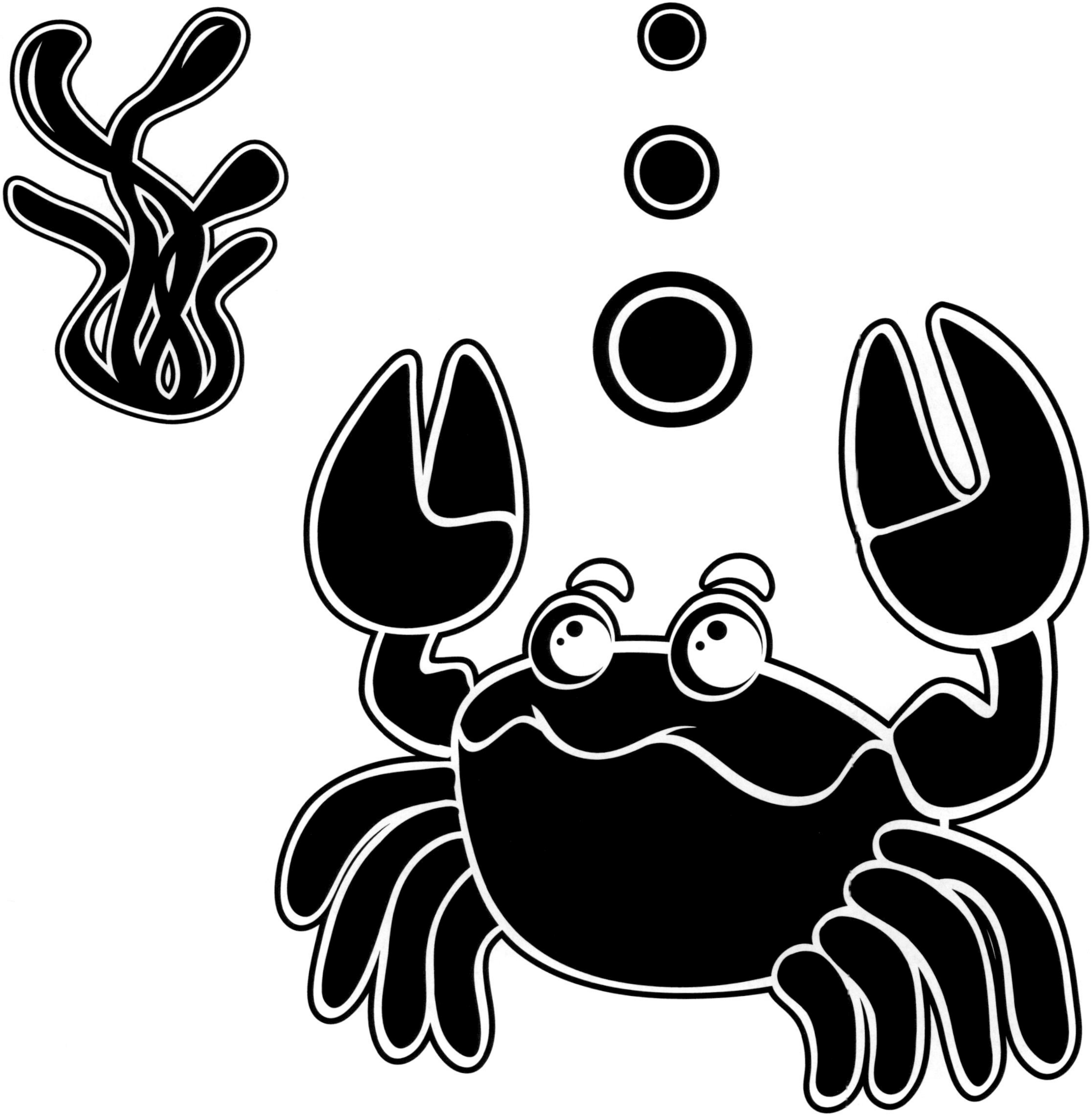

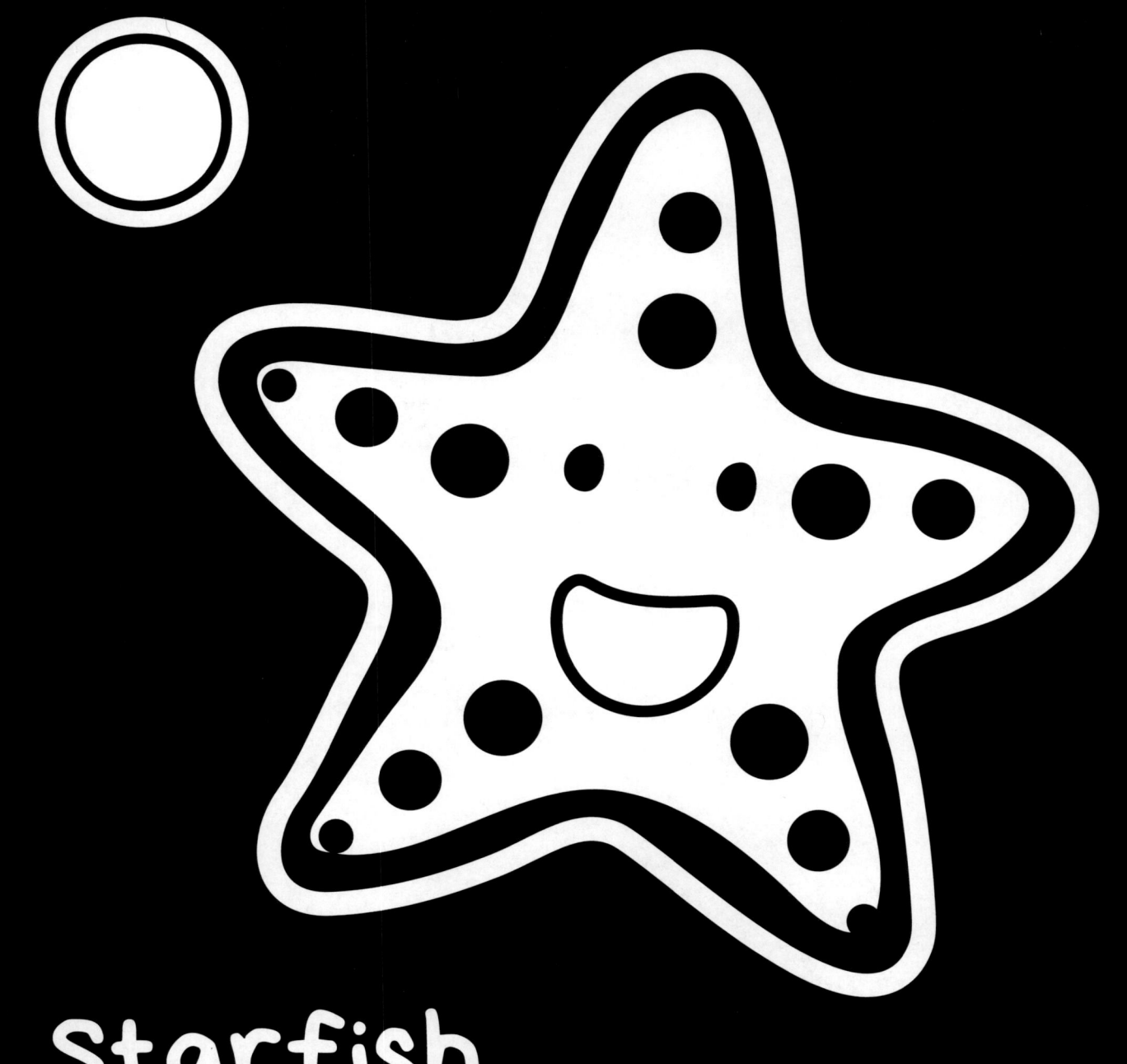

Starfish

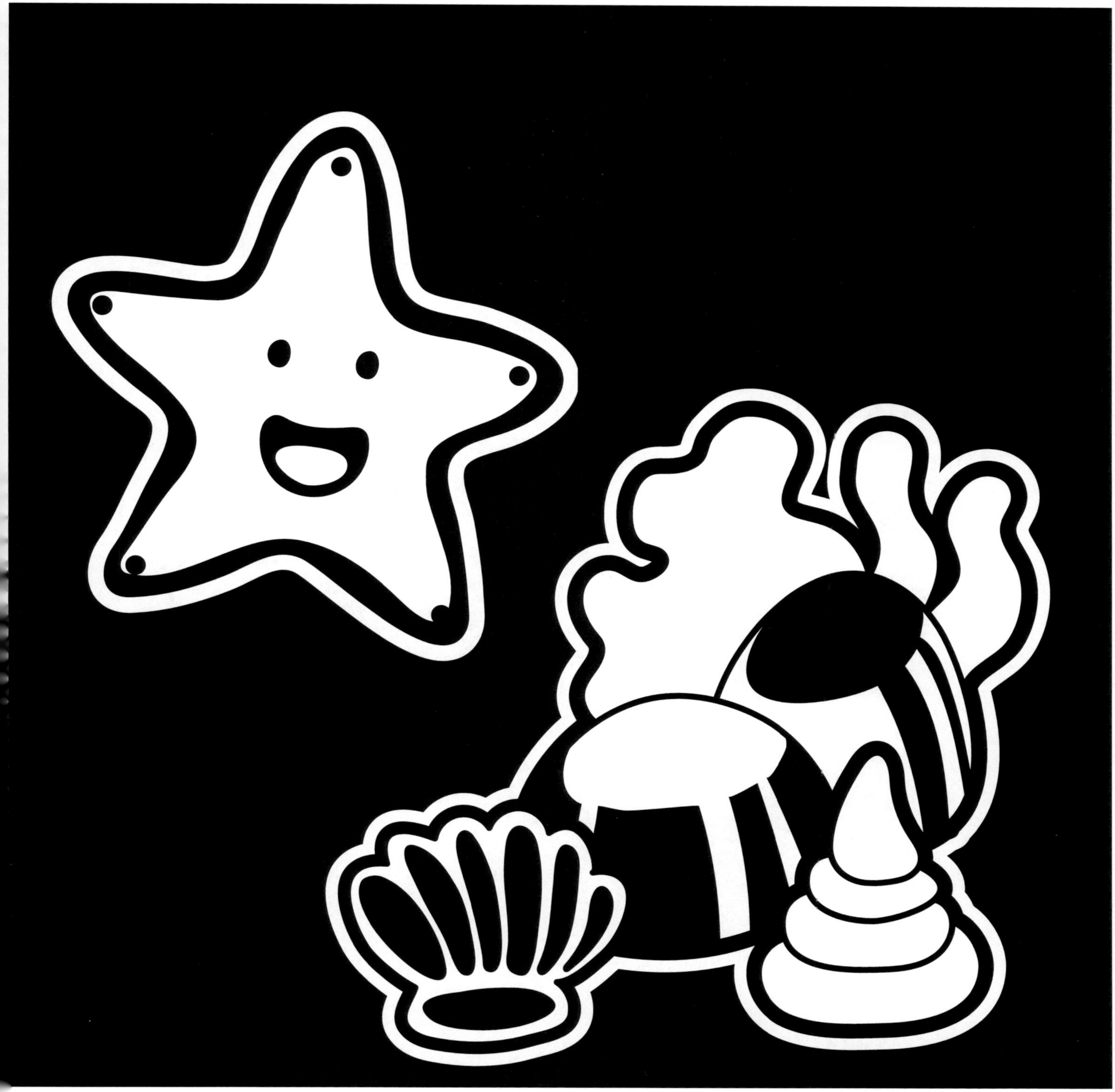

shark

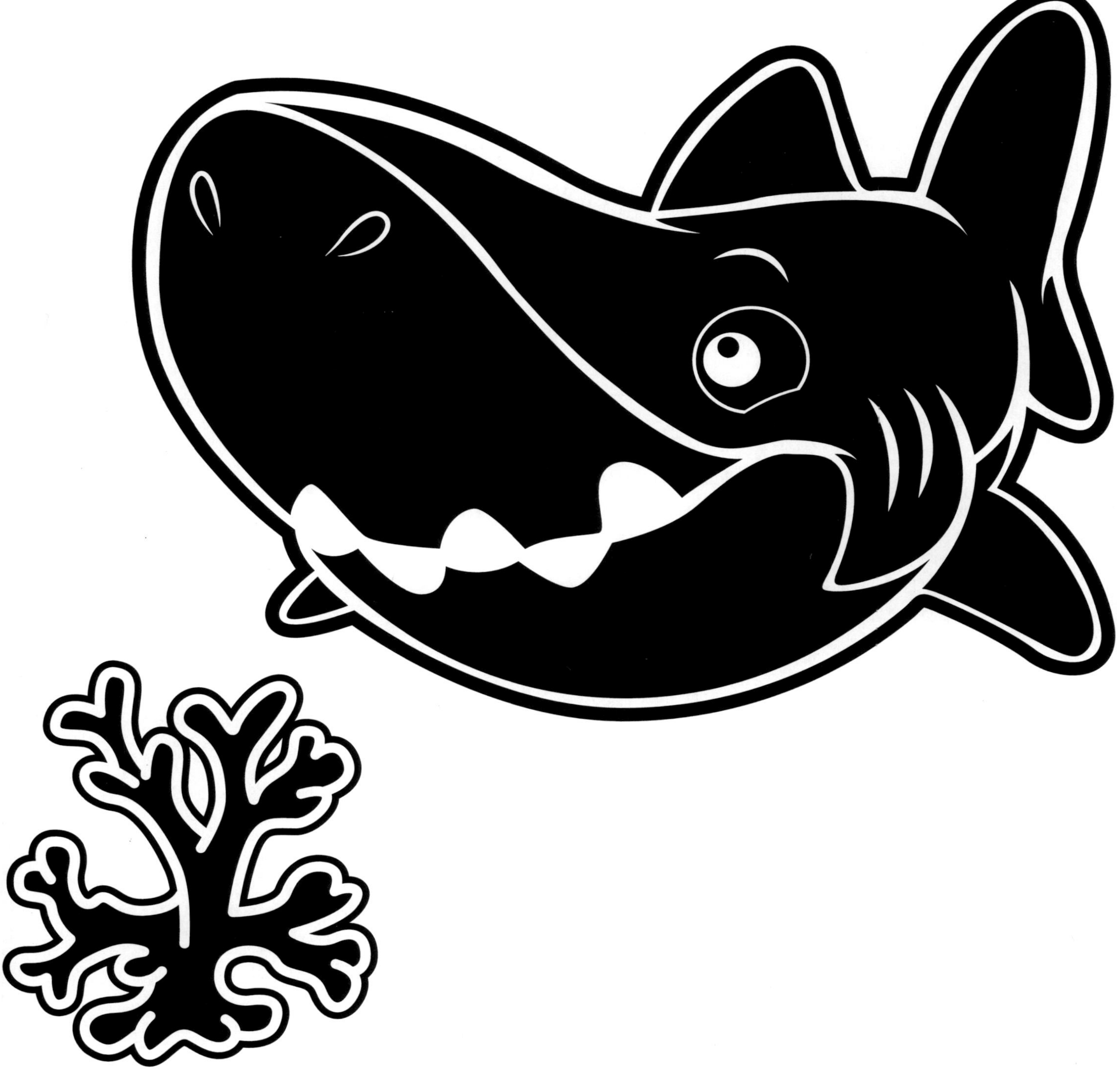

Stingrays

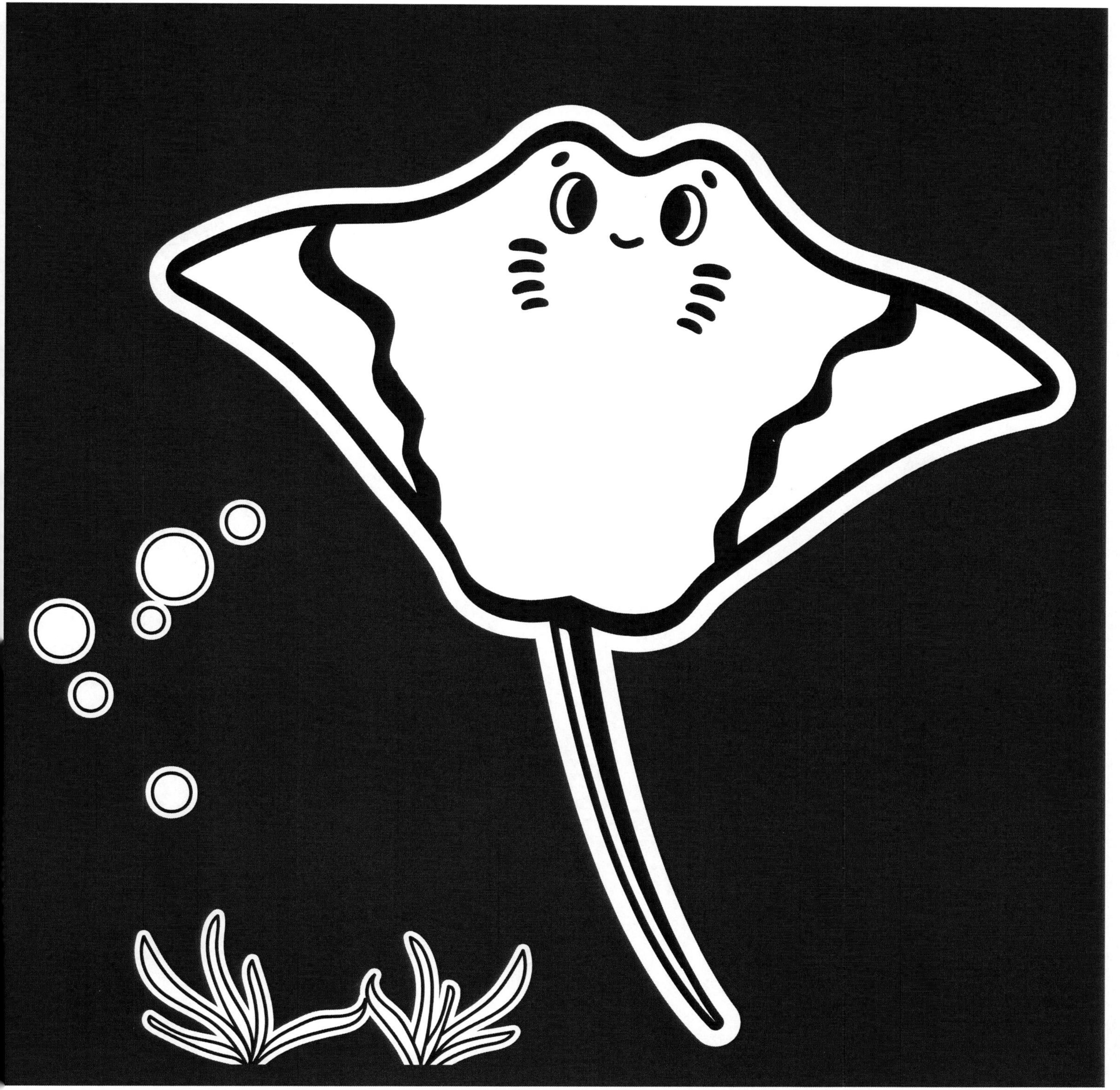

Jellyfish

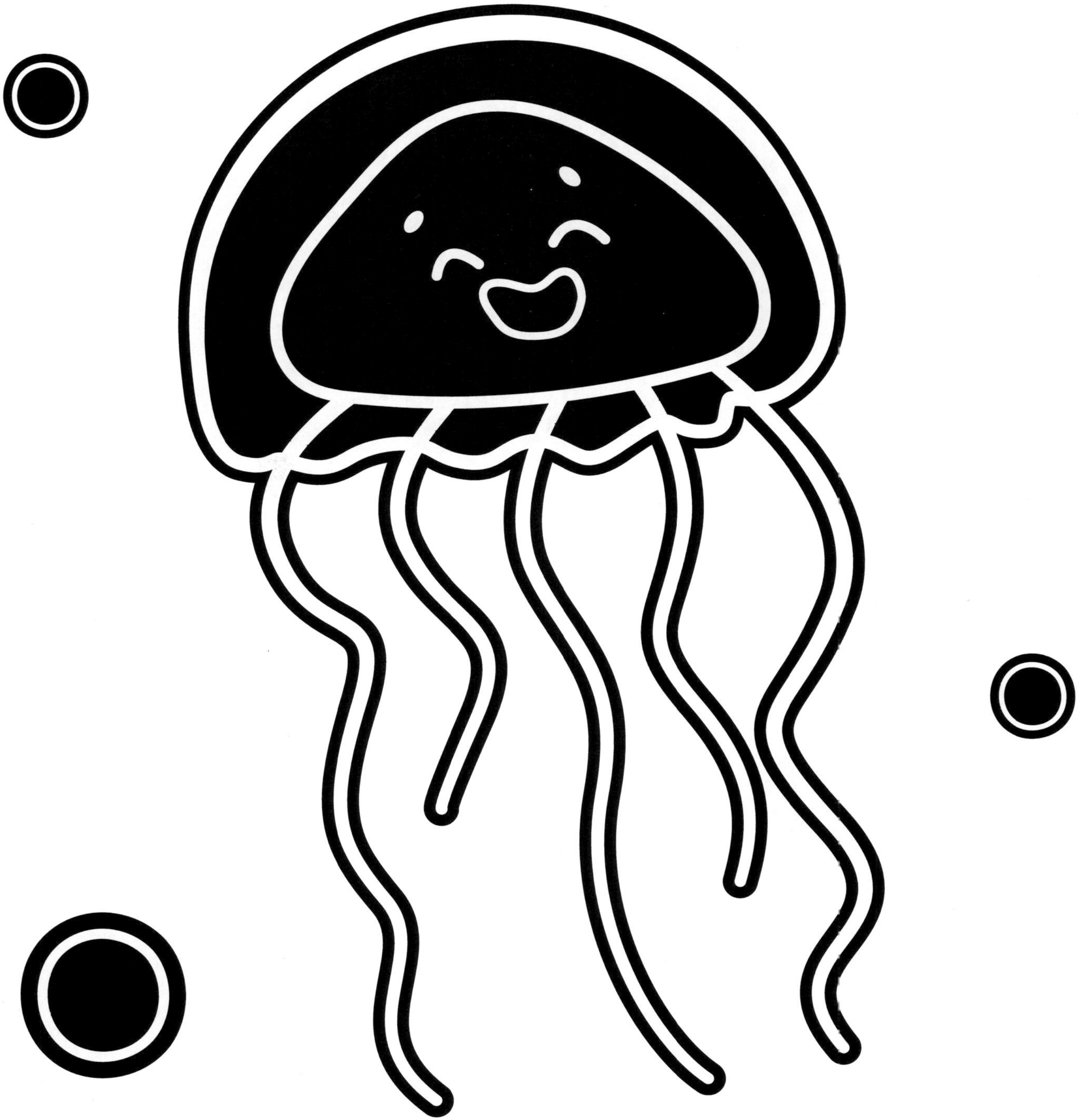

Whale

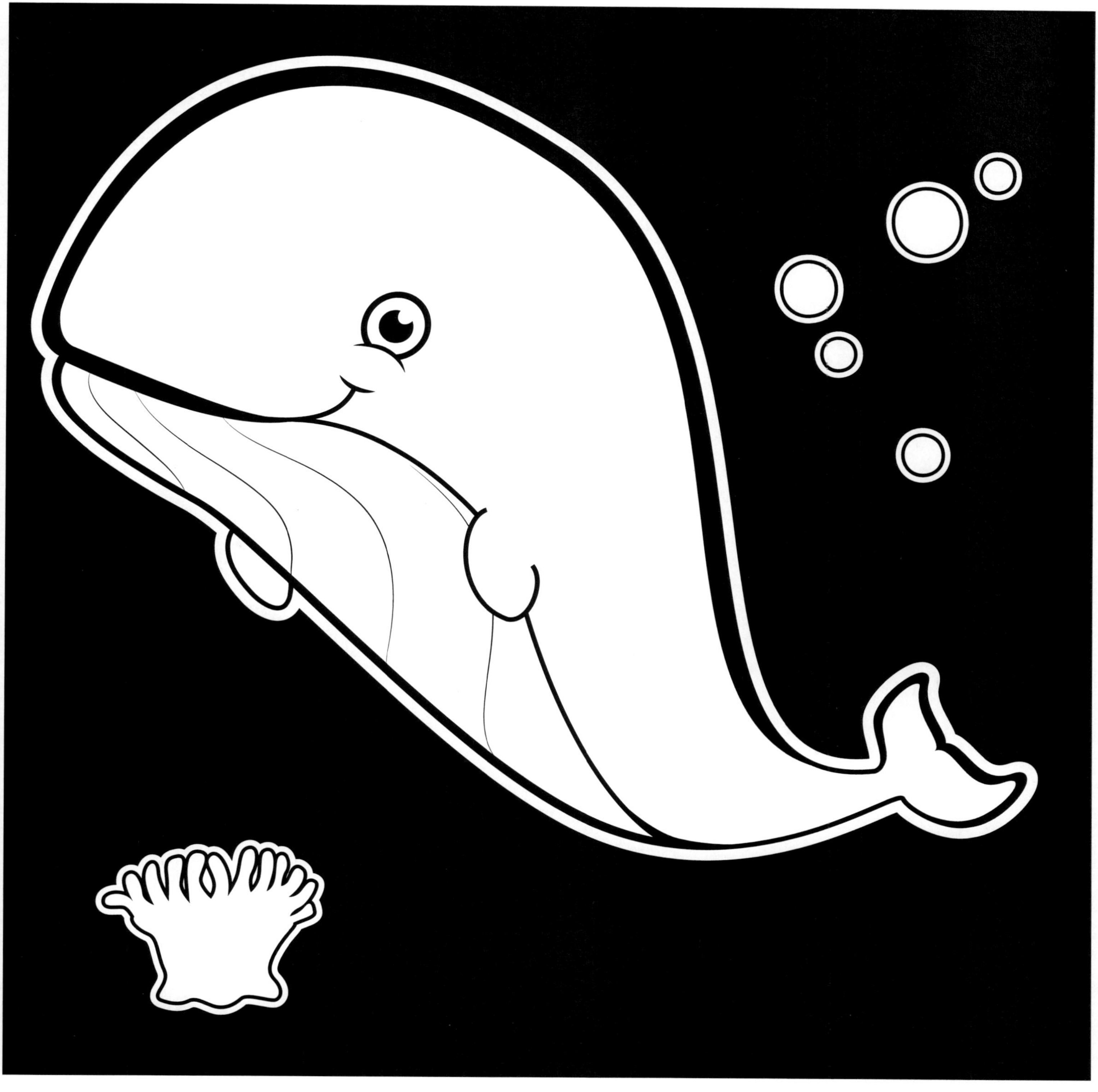

squid

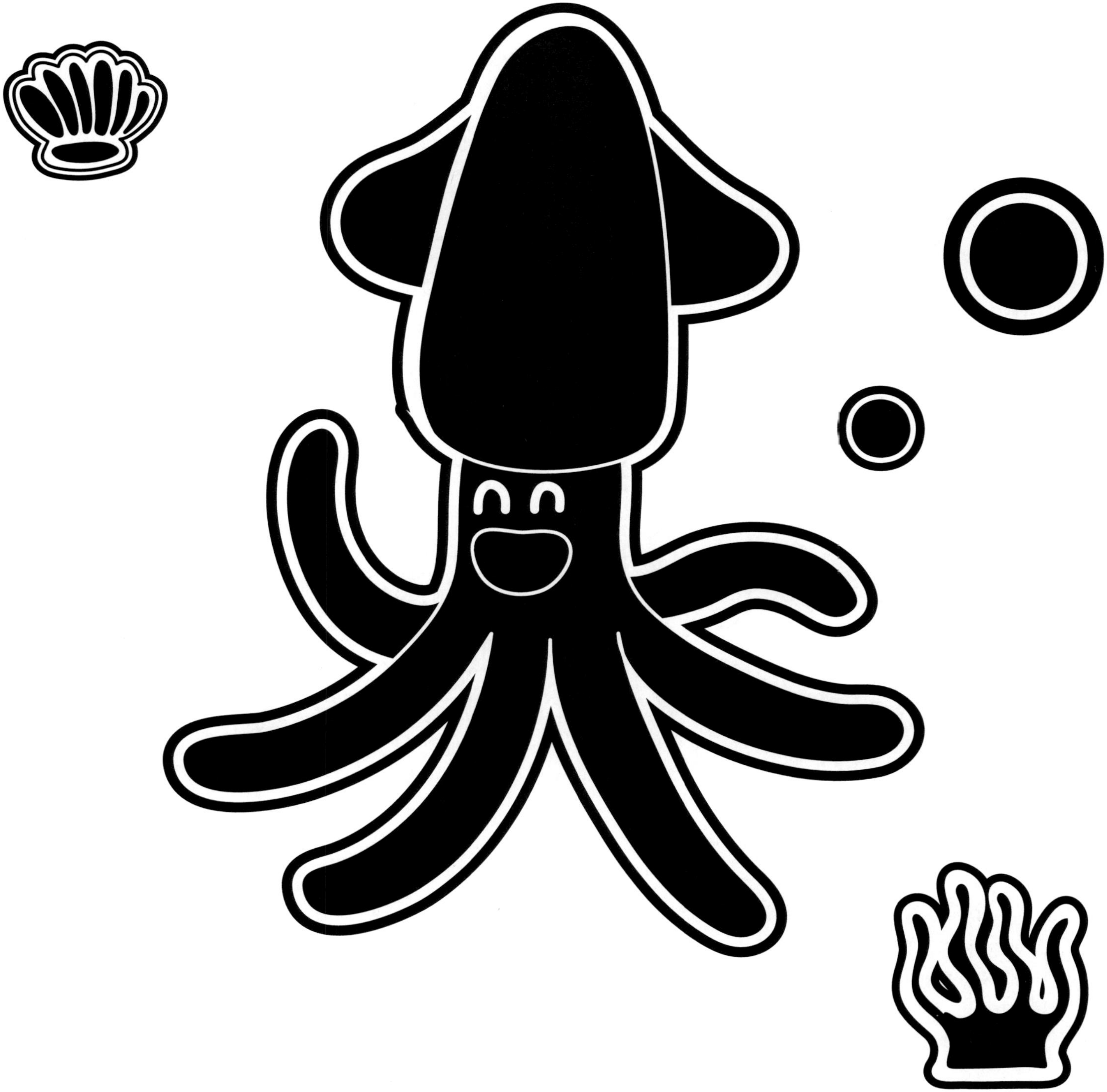

Lobster

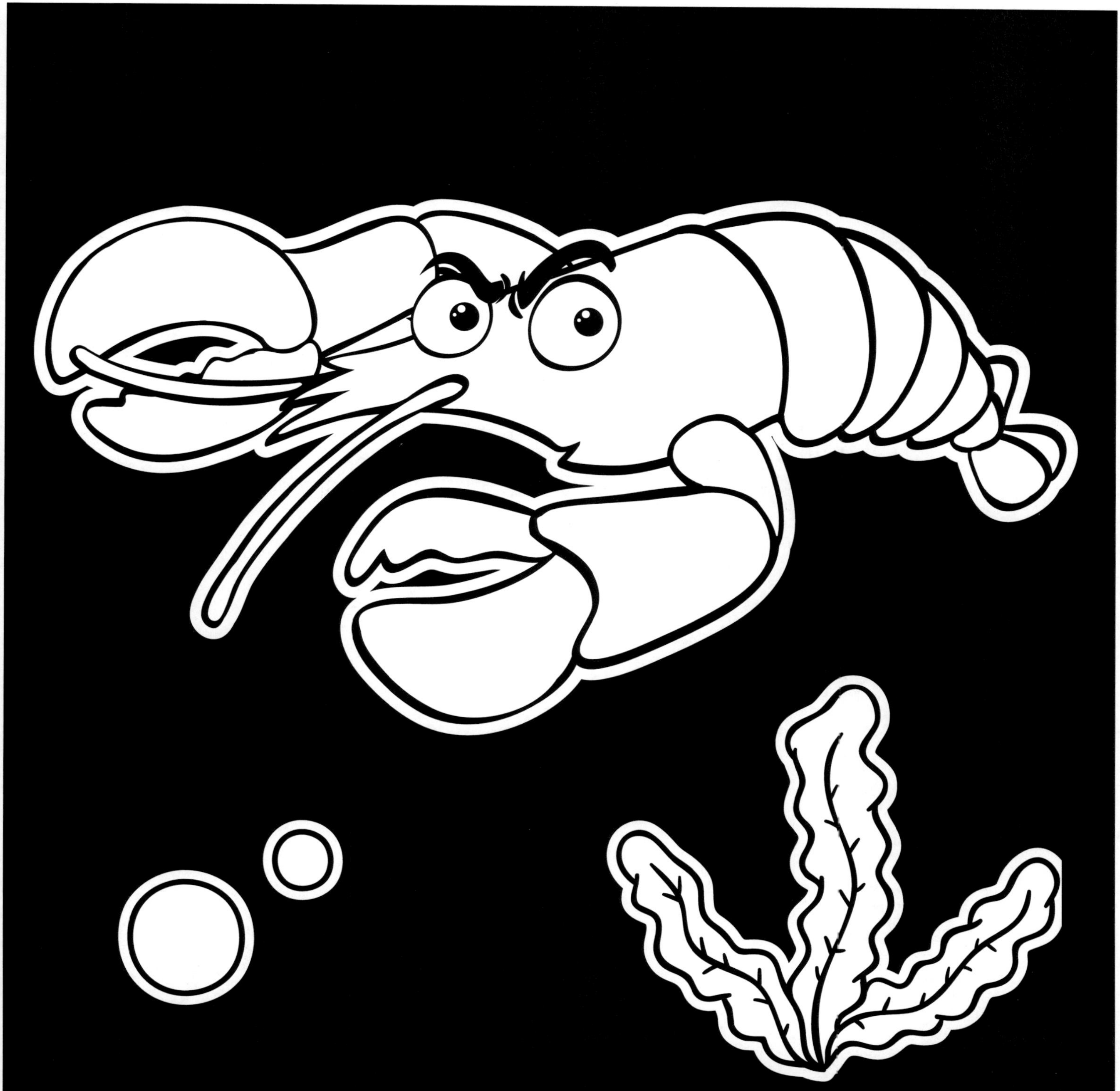

Prawn

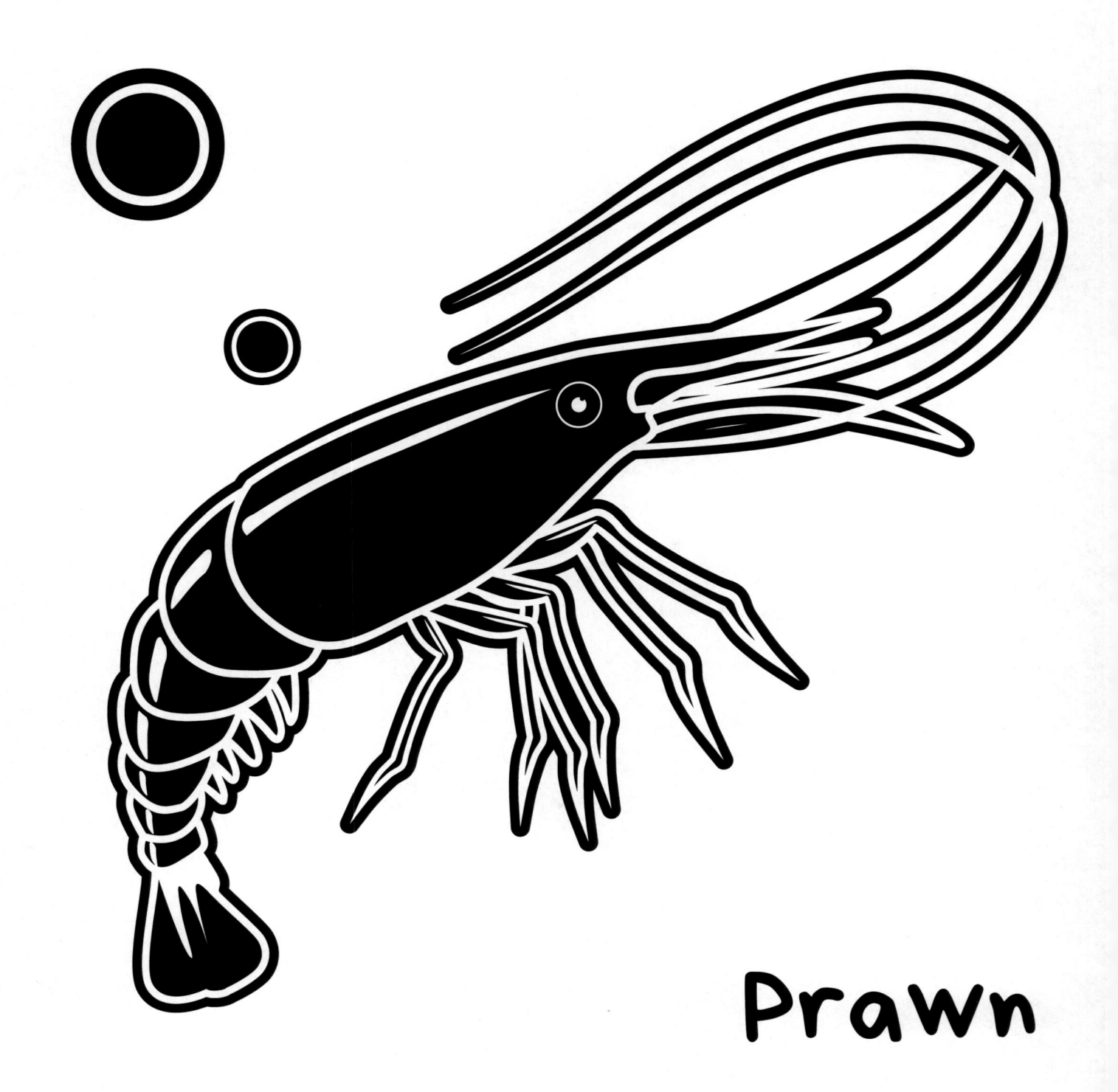

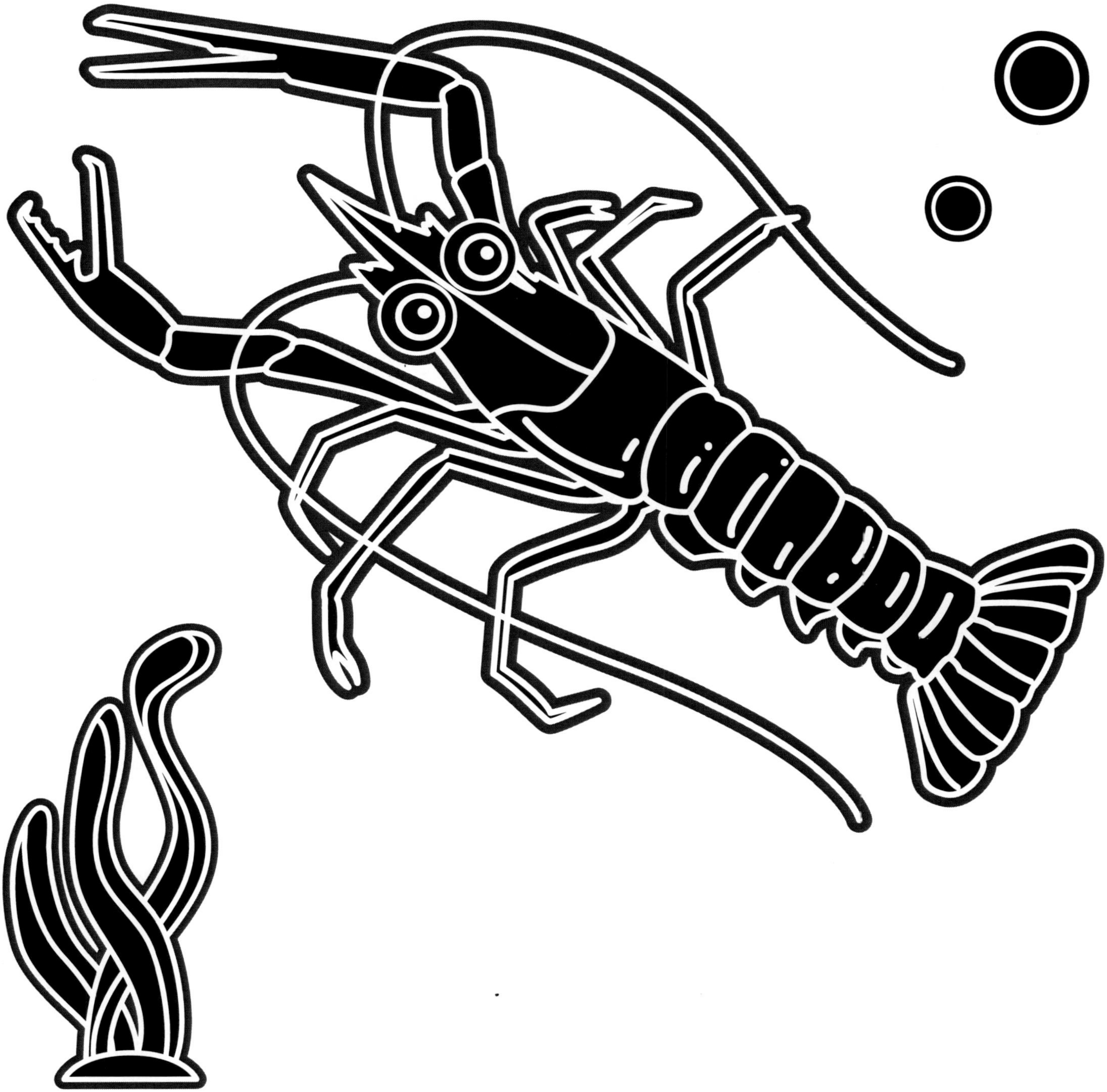

Eel

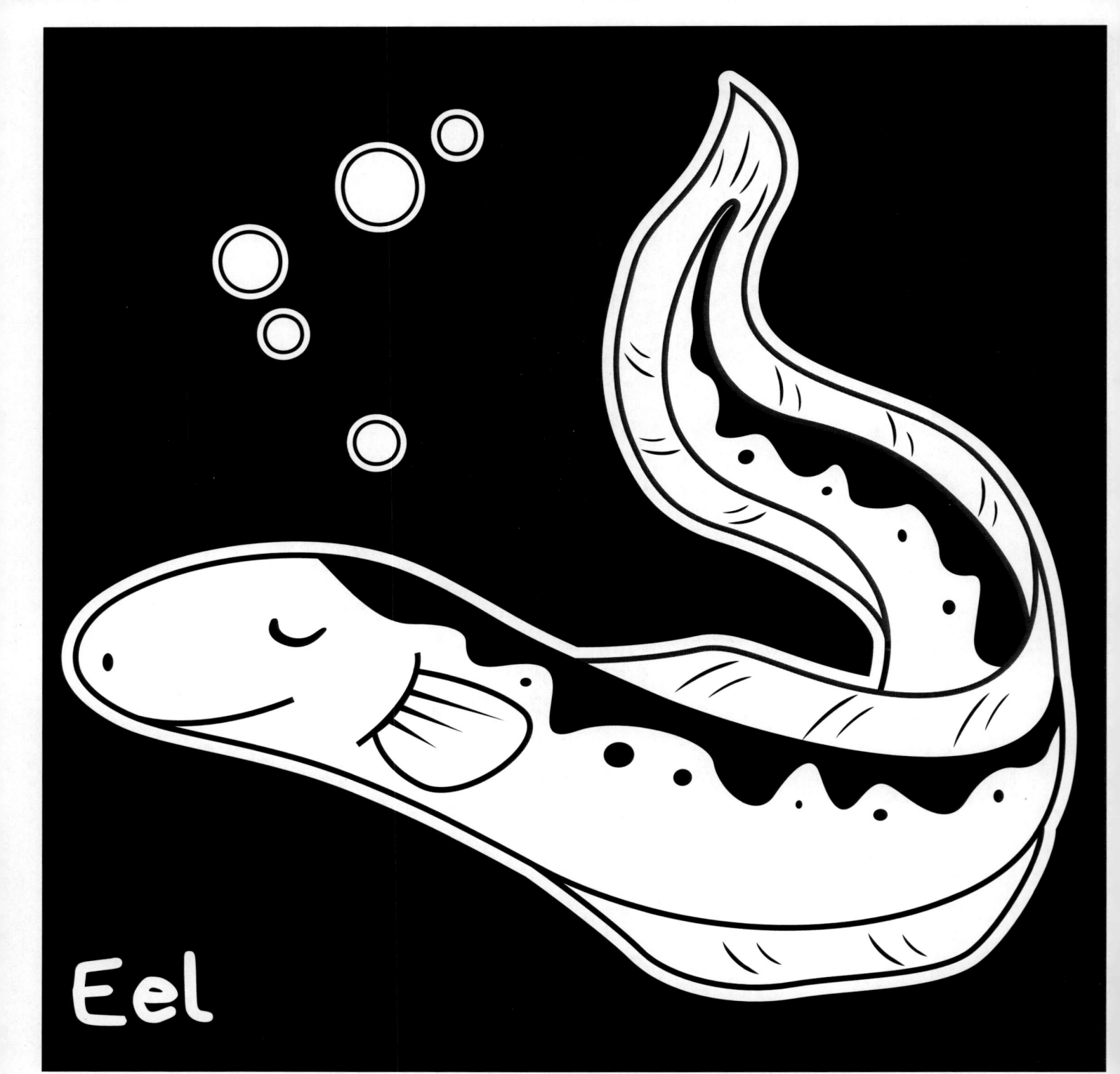

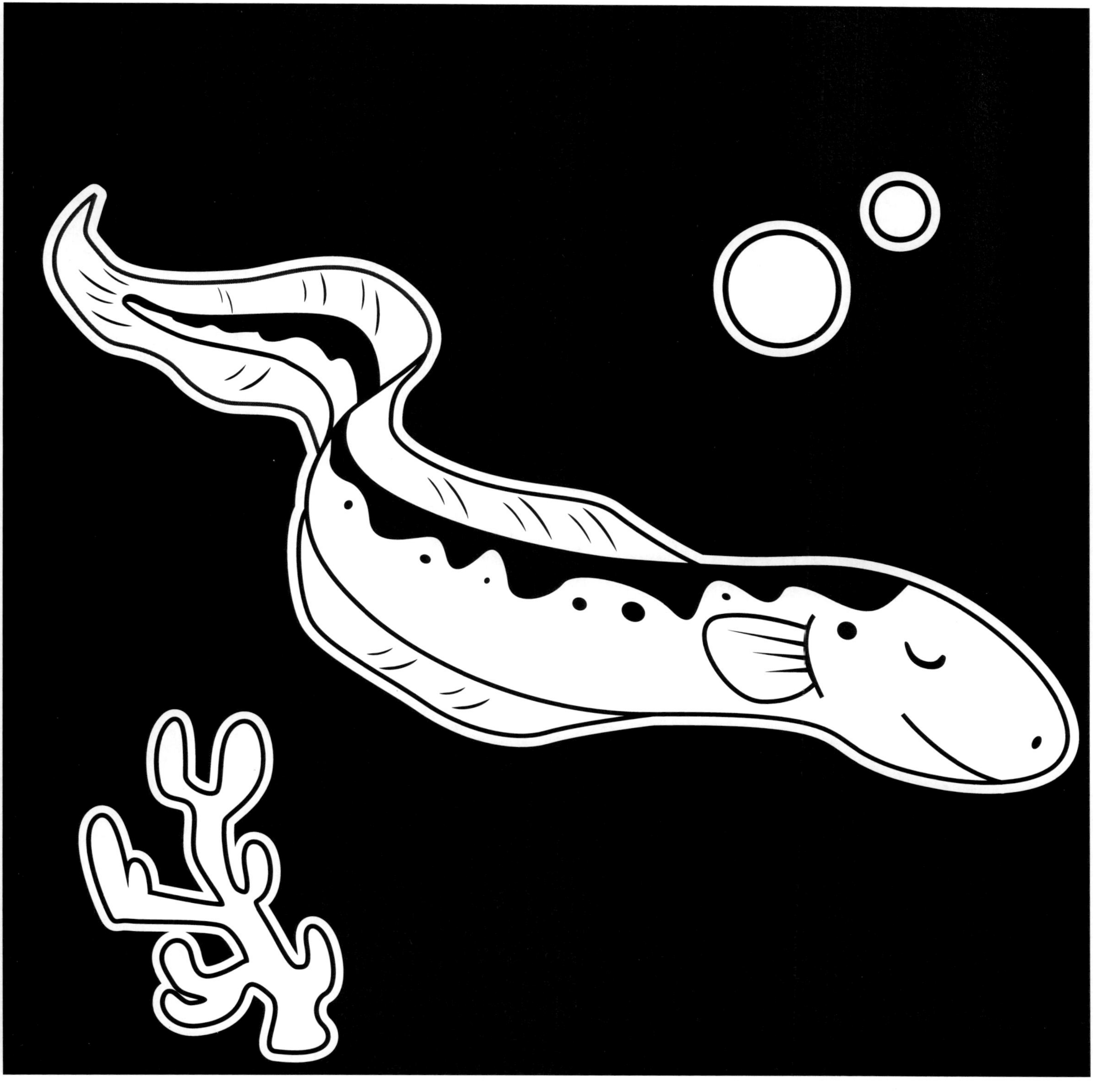

Orca

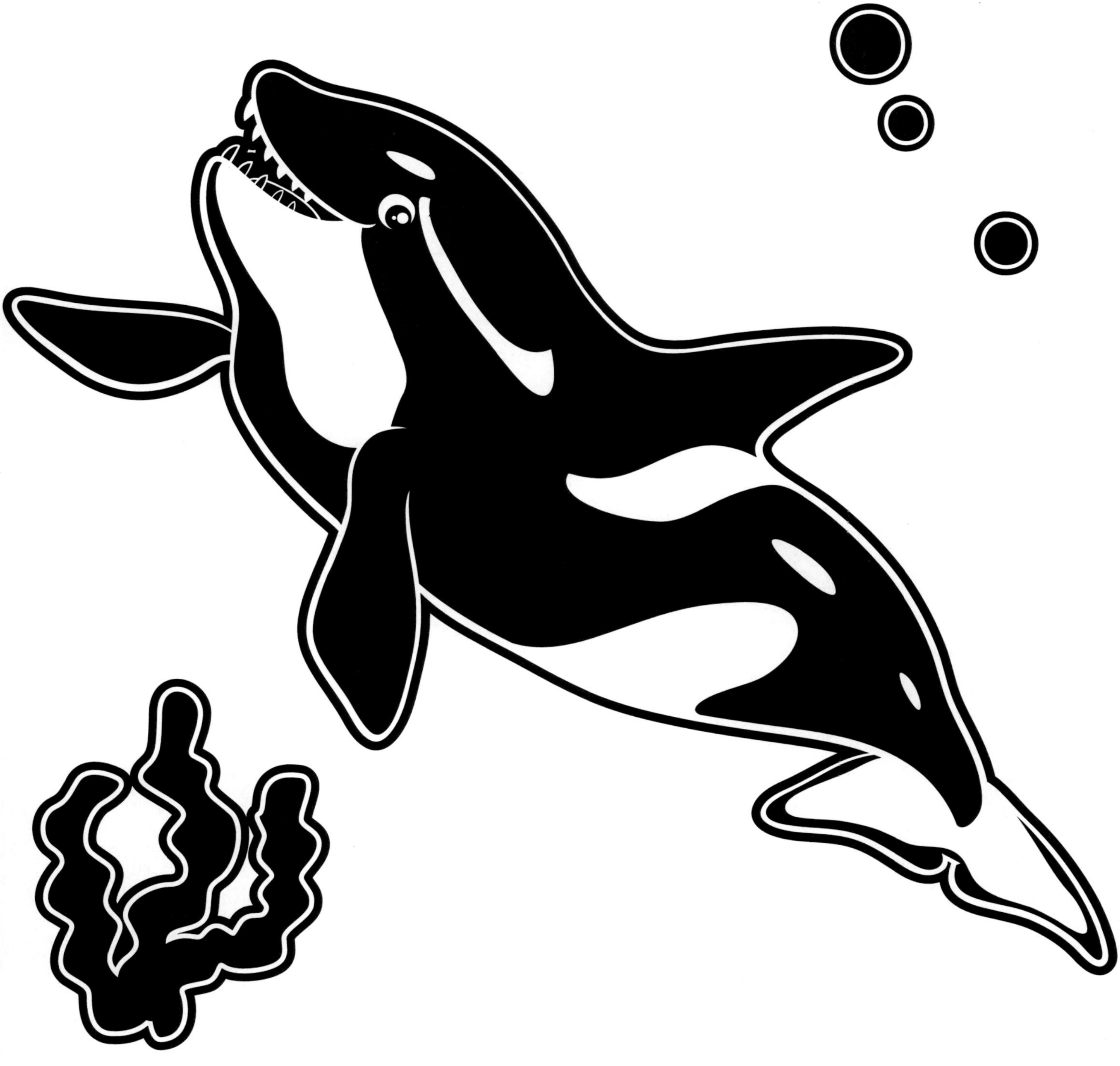

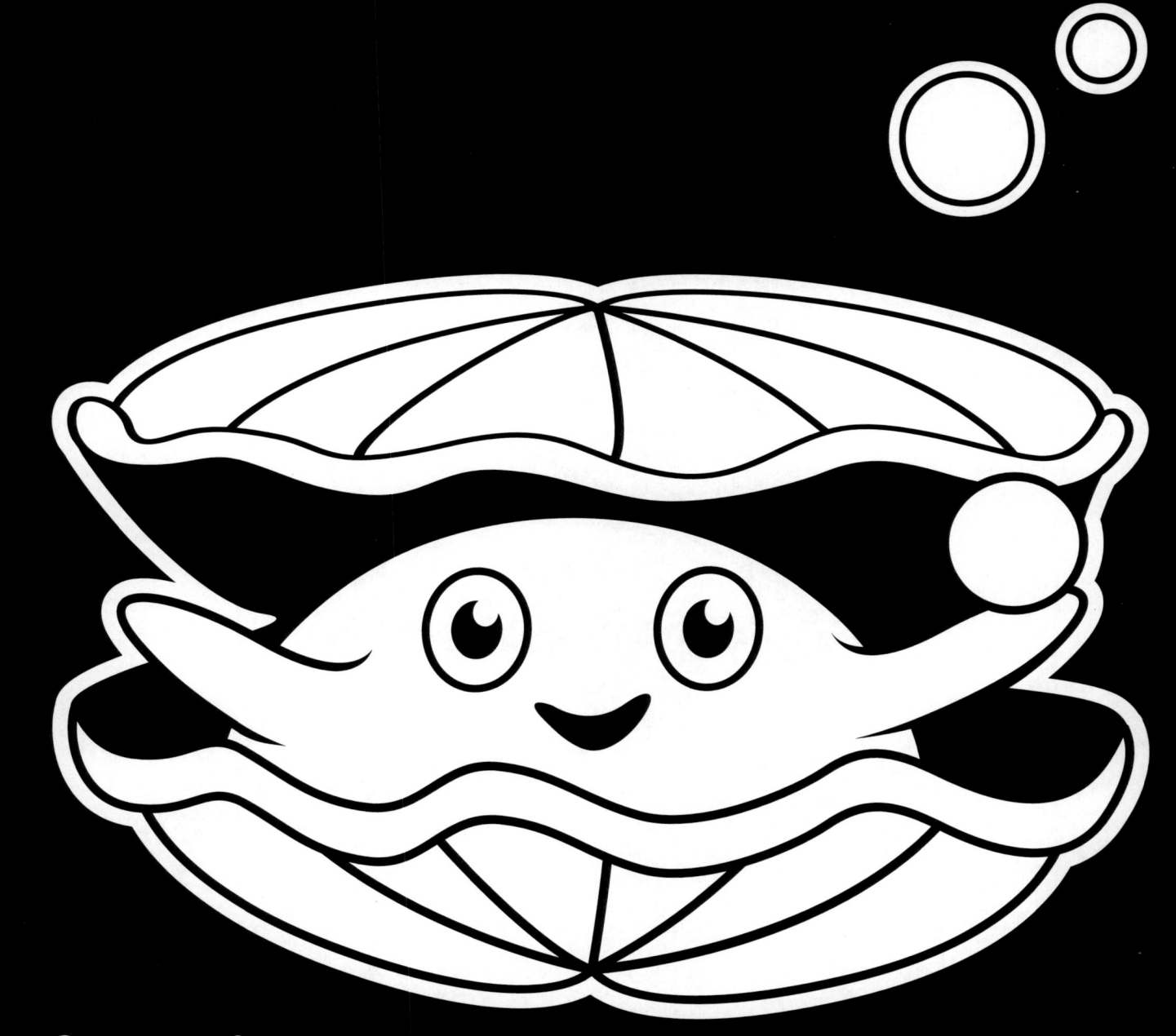

Oyster

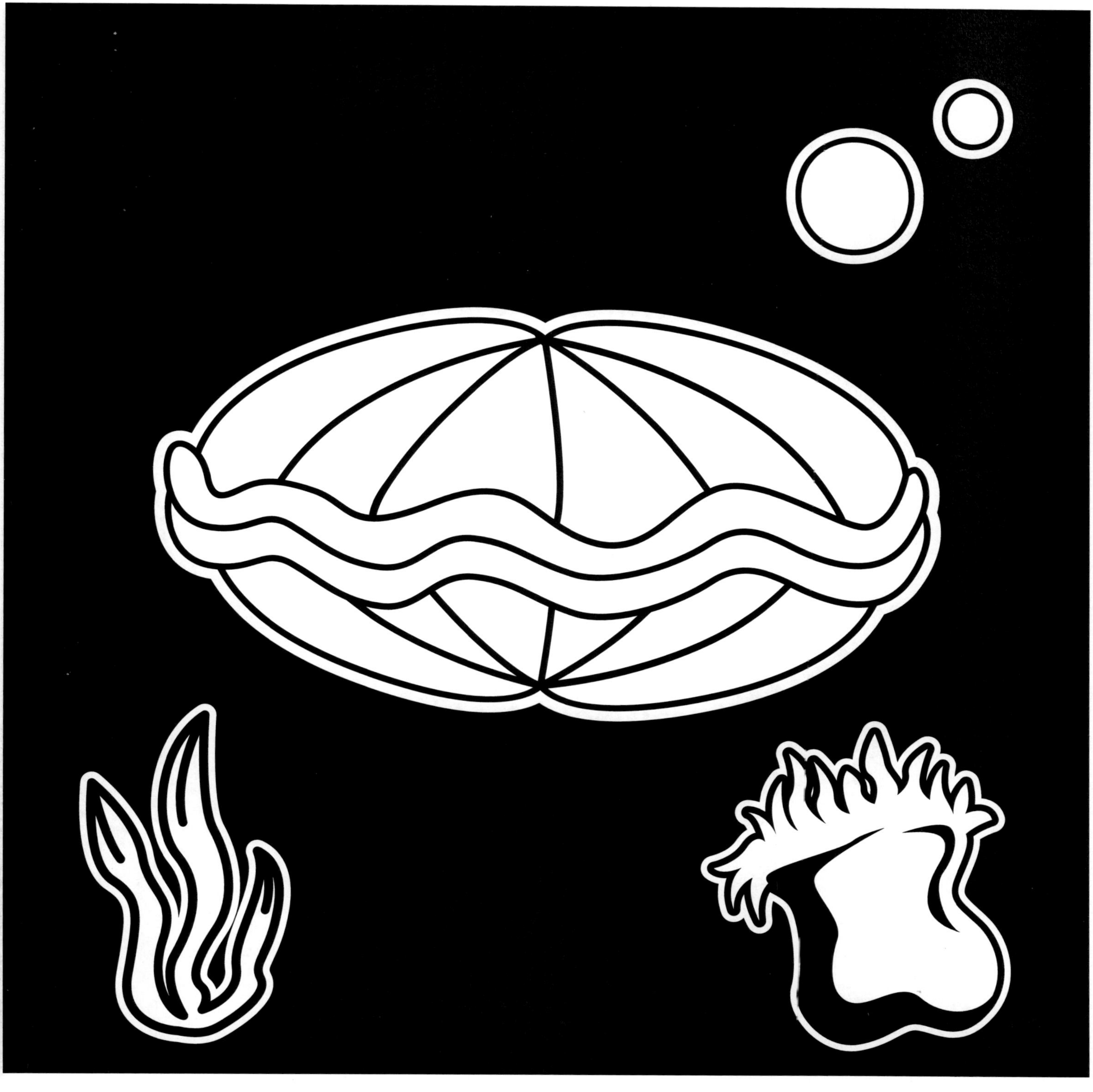

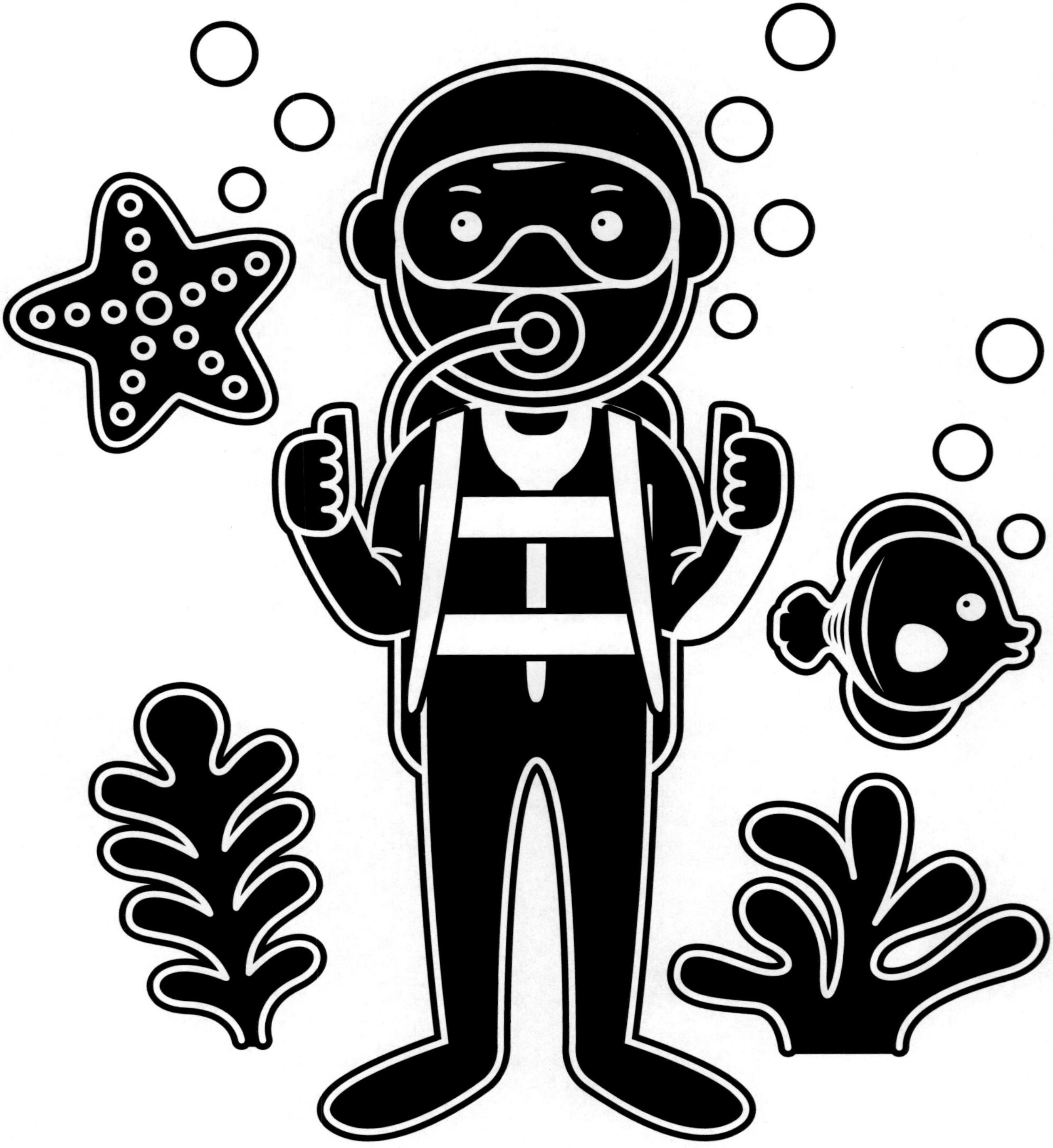

Did you like the book?

Please, leave feedback.

It helps the book stand out from the crowd.

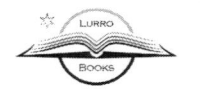

Made in United States
North Haven, CT
14 December 2021